FAVOR
DAILY

Poetry for the Soul Volume II

BY

MADAME BUTTERFLI

POEMS ARE IN ALPHABETICAL
ORDER

Peggy' for you
Thanks for
support
God Bless
~Madame
Butterfli

MADAMEBUTTERFLI.COM

PO BOX 34093 ST. LOUIS, MO 63134
WWW.MADAMEBUTTERFLI.COM

FAVOR DAILY: POETRY FOR THE
SOUL VOLUME 2/ MADAME
BUTTERFLI. – 2ND ED.

ISBN-13: 9780692260715

ISBN-10: 0692260714

Dedication

This book is dedicated to those
who I can depend on daily to
inspire me

They give me the best advice
without beating me up too badly,

Just know that I don't take it lightly

Prologue

I celebrate as I open my eyes

Appreciative of the good and the bad

What things are, what they are not

What things will be, what they will not be

Exhilarated for another day, another chance

Grateful for another opportunity, another breath

Lead me down the right path

Show me that which is good, take away

what is not

I am delighted to follow you

Another day

Gift

We receive each day an unrivaled
gift

Eagerly, I unwrap my present
wondering what I will get

It's a surprise to me when I see all
that my father has given to me

Love, happiness, peace of mind,
comfort during all of the hard times

Healing from sickness, provision to
no end, the unfailing trust of an
incorruptible friend

As I continue my day, the gifts
never cease

I lose count as I recollect all of the

marvelous things

Down I lie only to anxiously awake,
to unwrap the gift of another
beautiful day

A Smile

*People are all a blessing, greet
each one with a smile*

*You just may be able to turn
someone's day around*

*A smile is a symbol showing that
you care, a reflection of what's
inside*

*There is a window to your soul
when you smile with your eyes*

*It takes less effort to smile than to
frown*

*We can all make an effort to turn
someone's day around*

A Word

People will often forget what you
say, but remember how you make
them feel

Be careful with your words and
speak those that heal

We just may travel through the
valley with no kind assertion to be
heard

We all want to hear it, but no one
wants to say a word

Let your consideration show more
than your wrath

Be anxious to steer someone away
from the wrong path

What you sow into others will be

exchanged

You will receive happiness from
another life saved

Against the Tide

Boldness and revelation are your companions while going against the tide,

with an abundance of hope and a steady stride

Your destination may be far off, but your starting point is no longer visible

Returning is incomprehensible

You've come too far to throw in the towel

Do everything within your power except worry about how

As you progress, more revelation will come,

giving you the boldness to continue forth

With an abundance of hope and a steady stride,

It will only become natural to go against the tide

All That I Ask

*Just as the water covers the rocks
in a stream, I know that my
protector covers me*

*Hurt, danger, lies, and defeat, I
worry not because of the strength
that lies within me*

*I am able to withstand at whatever
cost, fully regaining what is lost*

*My trust is in the right place,
bitterness shall not destroy my
taste*

*I am overtaken by the sweetness
of your affection, my soul and my
being are not without the greatest
protection*

*I go forward each day with
renewed life, free from anger and
strife*

*I know that what's before me is
brighter than my past, guide me
through is all that I ask*

Balance

Pray for bliss and renewing of the
mind

Search within yourself and let your
anxieties unwind

Refuse to let other pull you into
their pit

Keep your thoughts high and with
your praises lift,

your spirit into the next dimension

Be free from worry, pain, and
tension

Seek to be balanced and keep your
load light

Don't hop onto someone else's
roller coaster ride

Be Kind

You never know what is going on in
someone's mind

Let your words be counted as good
and cause you to shine

You are only remembered by what
you say and your deeds

Encouraging someone else
increases your chances to succeed

We are only on this earth for a
moment, leave a lasting impression

Your thoughtfulness can change
someone's view of their own
reflection

You never know what is going on in
someone's mind

Always make an extra effort to be
kind

Be Whole

Be whole, with a well of happiness springing from your soul

Living our next life in paradise is the goal

Resist the urge to create heaven on earth at any cost

Reject what will cause your soul to be lost

Leave anger and contention at the gate

Walk with the intention of being great

Everything done in private will be revealed

Say yes to the right things, don't be fooled by a false shield

Be caring and kind not allowing unforgiveness to take root

Don't let bad apples spoil your fruit

*Think responsibly, we are only
accountable for what we do*

*Make good decisions to reach your
goal*

*Be whole, with a well of happiness
springing from your soul*

Beautiful Flowers

Take a look around and see the
bouquet, all of the colors that
surround us everyday

Every flower unique, no two are
exactly the same

Each one has a purpose and is
called by a different name

Predestined for greatness, no
matter from where they came

Planted with intention, to add color
to the lives of others

Our existence is not about
ourselves, but the positive change
that we bring

Our commitment to our sisters and
brothers make it all worthwhile

As we fulfill our aspirations, our
inner man smiles

Whether it's a cold winter night or the sun is beaming bright

You are surrounded by beautiful flowers that will bring joy into your life

The Beauty of God's Creation

There is such beauty in God's creation, person to person and nation to nation

We are all unique, yet similar at the same time

Many of the differences we create with our mind

In order to get along, we must find common ground

It's much easier than it may appear when we know our true selves and let go of fear

We find that together we can do more, spreading love and peace instead of war

Eliminating greed and taking care of our poor

Seeing purpose in ourselves and each other, regardless of race, creed, or color

We would be unstoppable only if

we recognized the beauty in God's creation

The Best

We have no control over what others may think, we can only be the best at what we were chosen to be

Gracefully we can sleep, as God above surrounds us with his peace

His love overshadows all fear,

we do not walk alone, he is always near,

Can't be seen, yet is not invisible, can't be touched, yet is felt,

as we are submitted and transformed, no longer governed by ourselves

We are only as good as our ears to listen, our souls quickened as we answer,

to be the best at what we are chosen to be,

*we have no control over what
others may think*

Better

What can I do today to be better than yesterday?

Follow God every step of the way

Keep a steady pace without moving with haste

Time will not wait for me to contemplate the why, where, how, and when

If he showed me before, he will again

I'll just focus on what he already has in place

Preparation is in the present for the rest of the race

Blessed Day

A blessed day awaits, don't
hesitate

Do not fear opposition, it is a sign
that you are on the right path

Consider yourself blessed when
there is an attack

Continuing to work only sets your
enemy farther behind

As you reach closer to your goals,
the hidden blessings of life begin to
unfold

The more you recognize the more
power you gain

Making irrelevant any heartache or
pain

An eternal flame overshadows
whatever darkness that may
appear

Quickly obliterating any fears

Don't hesitate, your blessed day awaits

Let nothing detour your faith

Blessings of a New Day Arise

Blessings of a new day arise along with us

Time to finish the undone, improve what was wrong

A chance to start over fresh after being down for so long

This day as you open your eyes, don't ignore the blessings of a new day, arise

Take the new opportunity that you tossed aside

Refine your goals, pursue your passions within

Move closer to the mark, start living again

Make a decision starting today, to live your life in a more fulfilling way

Breaking and Shifting

Just as if an earthquake has occurred, life is stirred

The breaking and shifting cannot be denied

Transformation will not hide, begin to roll with the tide

Just as the blooming of a flower, difficulty displays your power

It is impossible to return to what is faded

Avoid being jaded, renew your mind and yourself

New knowledge is new wealth

Breaking and shifting cannot be denied

Refuse to be tied to what is out of date

Be receptive, trusting that all things fall into place

Chains in Your Mind

Let go of yourself, break the chains
in your mind

Abandon your worries and leave
uncertainty behind

Become absolutely sure about the
future that is in store

Don't allow distractions to take you
on a detour

Spend each day striving towards
your goals

We each have our own story to be
told

Our paths may cross, but no two
are alike

You will be discouraged by looking
at another man's plight

Don't waste time comparing, we
are diverse by intent

Self-improving according to your own purpose is time better spent

Search within your soul and see what you hear

Break the chains in your mind, it will all become clear

Created With Intent

You are unique, one of a kind

Created with intent to change
someone's life

Don't take the resistance that you
face for granted

With every triumph, another good
seed is planted

Your trials are not to benefit your
own need, but for everyone who is
willing to take heed

We have everything right in front
of us to succeed

Just open your eyes and take hold,
wisdom is worth more than gold

None of our experiences are alike

Learn from someone else so that
you too don't have to pay the price

We are all unique, one of a kind

*Created with intent, to change
someone's life*

Collapse or Stand

Choose to build on honesty and truth

What is built on lies will collapse, not because of another, but by its own traps

Deal fairly and wisely, you will have friends for life

Selfish ambitions will only stir up strife

Seek direction daily, be not lost, but found

We live not only for ourselves, but those around

Lead by example, you know who is watching

Our next generation, what will they learn?

What will they do when it is their turn?

Will they collapse or stand?

Dig Deeper

What you see at the surface is not
true at the depth

Like a mirage in the desert,
illusions arise

Misguiding the unaware near the
cliff-side

Focus and remain on course,
driven by instruction directly from
the source

Treasure is buried and difficult to
find

Do the work and dig deeper, or you
may as well be blind

Search for more than what appears
to be

At the surface, it's not always what
it seems

Excellent

*You cleanse my mind and remove
all doubt,*

renew my spirit so that I can shout

*Thank you for your sacrifice, filling
my life with joy*

*My thoughts are pleasant now that
I am in your presence*

*Keep me near to thee, inhabiting
with the free*

On one accord with your will

*Continuously pour into me your
spirit of excellence*

So that I will be just as you are

Excellent

Experience

Expertise comes from experience

Keep your eyes open and your ears tuned in

Ups and downs, highs and lows, formulate our lives causing us to grow

We can't understand what we don't see

First-hand or second-hand

Find the silver lining regardless of what you may think

Stay away from the deep end of negativity

Once you fall into it, it's difficult to get back up

Remain balanced if times get rough

*Experience makes experts, all
things turn out for the best*

*You are never alone during your
trials and your tests*

Faith

My load is a lot easier since I do
not carry it all

It's good to have someone on
which you can call

Any time of day, morning or night

When things are well, or not going
quite right

I abandon every weight that ties
me down

Permitting me to stand without my
head hanging down

I am free to sing, dance, and shout

From every perplexing
predicament, I've made it out

When life gets heavy, don't forget
to pray

Your faith will carry your burdens
from day to day

Faith to Finish

*Have enough faith to finish what
you start*

*Discouragement will come and go,
don't take it to heart*

*If there is no one to cheer in the
stands, keep on pushing and leave
it all in God's hands*

*It takes courage to fight in the
dark, continue to move towards
the mark*

*Take pleasure in a beautiful
masterpiece at the end*

*You'll understand why it was such
a struggle to win*

The Fire

Trials of life will only make us
stronger

Learning and remaining positive
will prevent us from staying in
them longer

So many things about ourselves we
have yet to learn

During the process, we must allow
what is detrimental in our lives to
burn

No matter how difficult it gets,
triumph is on the other end

Face your fears and your faults
with vigor to win

We all come out of the fire in due
time

Just as pure gold, our victory
causes us to shine

For You

*If you seek God, he will find you
where you are, there is no place
that is too far*

*Whether is the highest lookout or
the lowest place, he will never fail
to meet you face to face*

*Even if he does not visibly move,
God has not forgotten about you*

*Never be afraid of being left
behind, things will not happen
according to your time*

*Patiently wait, don't give in to
worry or stress, take a moment
and enjoy the rest*

*Like a flood, God's favor will rush,
you will soon forget all of the fuss*

*Say in faith with the right attitude,
knowing that what is to come was
designed just for you*

Forgetful Heart

A forgiving heart is a forgetful heart

Burying animosity will tear your life apart

Be swift to forgive and to also learn a lesson

Count every offense as a blessing

You gain knowledge from experience, learn how to love from pain

All the way around, forgiveness is a gain

Keep your heart and mind free from stress

By harboring strife, you will digress

Remember that a forgiving heart is

a forgetful heart

*Don't allow animosity to tear your
life apart*

Go!

Many wonderful gifts await

All from He who determines our fate

Give, ask, trust, and believe

Having assurance that you will receive

It is a privilege to walk in the light

All that is shaded becomes illuminated, every twist is aligned,

Making it easy to reach your destination in record time

As we forgo our will, our gifts fall in line

Good and perfect, much too exquisite to purchase

Awaiting those who will respond to His command to "Go!"

God's Love and Protection

*My soul awaits your excellent
expression of love*

*Grateful for your divine protection
from above*

*You see the unseen and even feel
what I have felt*

*I take comfort in knowing that God
is my help*

*Everything good comes from Him,
that's why I trust when chances
are slim*

*I will not fear because of his divine
protection from above*

*All a part of his excellent
expression of love*

God Speaks

When everything around you
seems bleak,

God will always speak

No situation is too great or too
small

God is the problem solver of them
all

Cast all of your cares and burdens
on him, they will become light

Stand on God's word and continue
to fight

Our weapons you cannot see, only
feel the power therein

It is not your battle it is God's who
rises within

When things are the worst and

everything around you is bleak

*Trust and know that God will
always speak*

God's Time

My watch is set to God's time

My steps are ordered and I am
lead by the Divine

Anything to the contrary, I bind

I will not stray far from the line

Within his safety, victory is mine

All things revealed and received in
due time

My thoughts are aligned

I will keep my eyes opened and be
aware of the signs

Grateful that my God is so kind

Walking this path I truly find,
happiness

and a heart that is sublime

*With everything fulfilled according
to his time*

Grow

*Of myself I freely give, so that I
may be restored*

*Just as the transition of a
streaming river, constantly
renewed is the life of a giver*

*Stagnation breeds impurity, seek
fluidity*

*An open hand is always
replenished, you reap what you
sow*

*A liberal heart is never empty,
limitless love will flow*

*Seek to give just as you receive
and consistently*

GROW

Good Fruit

Let our lives produce an abundance
of good fruit,

Sweet and picturesque, our trees
are healthy from the root

Our ground is watered by our
prayer, fertilized by our
supplication

Our branches are pruned by God's
word

Let the thought of barrenness of
our tree be absurd

We can withstand the winter of our
lives

For in the spring, our flowers
bloom beautifully and bright

Cease to worry, in due time, your
labor will produce an abundance of

fruit

Sweet and picturesque, if your tree is healthy from its root

His Love Endures

Dance and sing, for the Lord is
good

Rest peacefully, for his love
endures

Lift your voice, raise your hands

All things work together for his
plan

The righteous believe and are
never forsaken

Though goodness does not appear,
we are not shaken

Our very being lies with our Father,

who sovereignly reigns with all
power

The wicked devices of man, cannot
stand

We conquer all through his name

Victory we proclaim

Dance and sing, for the Lord is good

Rest peacefully, his love always endures

If You Dare

*Allow love to flow from you, if you
dare*

*Touch the people that you meet
here and there*

*Don't be afraid to show others that
you care*

*Circumstances of life are not
always fair*

*You never know what pain they
bear*

True consideration is rare

*Take off the layers, no one wants
to see you put on an "air"*

*Your testament of hope, be willing
to share*

*Allow love to flow from you, if you
dare*

Jesus Loves Us

Jesus loves us in spite of our faults

In our weakness, we are made strong

Nothing is too great or small

Take it to the cross, He's covered it all

Surrender at let your mind be at ease

He will keep you in perfect peace

King of Kings

*I will lift my voice to you and sing,
"All praises to the king of kings!"*

*Your power and might flow like a
stream*

*You give me wings as an eagle,
victory over all evil*

I will bless your holy name

*The righteous proclaim, "He is
good! His mercy endures forever!"*

*I will look to you for eternity, your
love never fails*

*No matter what may come against
me, with God, I prevail*

*I will lift up my voice and sing, "All
praises to the king of kings!"*

Laughter

*Laughter is medicine, good for the
soul*

*Keep the heart of a child you grow
old*

*The stressors of life will always try
to take control*

*Don't allow agitation to overthrow
the radiance that streams from
your heart*

*Dance, laugh, and sing, joy to
many you will bring*

*Being lively and playful doesn't
cost a thing*

*Fill your days with positive change
by letting your frustrations go*

Don't be afraid to roll with the flow

Liberty's New Song

Liberty sings a new song

She has extended its verses,
making it beautifully long

She dances leaps in harmony with
the strings,

Smiling and laughing, her soul is
now free

As her feet land, they tap to the
beat of their own drum

methodically, just as her last
victory was won

Just as the mountains and valleys,
Victory sings high and low

Then, attaining her balance and
flowing into a pacifying alto

As the horns play, she chants
continuously, joyously of her
unimpeded sovereignty

Listen

Learn every day from what you encounter

Secrets are revealed if you pay attention

Be slow to speak and quick to listen

Your thoughts can be confirmed or put to rest

You may obtain all of the answers for your test

Even a fool is counted wise when he is quiet

One can easily subdue what could become a riot

Be a listener and learn from what you encounter,

willing to accept knowledge and power

Living Water

Living water fills my soul,

Every inch of it becomes new,
forcing out the old

I imagine it as being an ocean
where I can swim, covering my
being and removing my sins

If living water was a shower, I
would be tempted to rinse in it
every hour

I sometimes wish that living water
was a fountain

I would continuously fill my cup as
if it were Ice Mountain

More conveniently this water
comes simply when we ask

Therefore, we are able to
indefinitely

*bask in the radiance and goodness
of true life,*

Given to all, by his stripes

Look, Listen, and Live

Have your way in my heart, my
life, and my soul

Cleave to my side, keep me from
going cold

My God, my center, my source and
strength

Replenish me as a fountain, as I
sow your gifts

Your Holy Spirit flowing is pure
delight, steadily increase my
appetite

I long to dwell in the midst of your
glory

As I experience your touch, I can
relay my story

There is one who holds all power in
his hands

Look, listen, and live; he never
takes away, but gives

His abundance is over what you could ever ask

Surrender and he will guide you through your divine task

The Loops of Life

*When you don't understand the
loops of life
trust that God is always right*

*All things are coming together for
those who love Him*

*The way is being guided when you
seem lost,
giving you the courage to fight at
all costs*

*Like a flood, God's love will abound
turning every negative situation
around*

*Don't be discouraged by the loops
of life*

*They just may be a detour from a
pitfall*

or dead end

Continue to trust that you are

guaranteed to win

The Master's Blueprint

The mission that was deposited in my heart was designed exclusively for me

I was created with intent, no other will fit

My lines and angles were perfectly patterned for the master's blueprint

So look at me and know that in spite of what you think, I am who God created me to be

Strategically planted in time and place to walk purposefully in His plan

My destiny cannot be overtaken by man, it is in the master's hands

Morning Song

The birds sing a different song as each morning awakes

Every day has a new rhythm, new lyrics, and spoken truths ready to unfold

We either dance to or against the beat

Our minds control our feet, fluid or decreased, on which our hilarity depends

Will joy win? Or, will the morning song be subdued?

You choose

Mountains Move

Mountains are high, but they will move

We can go wherever we choose

Take the scenic route or the freeway

Whatever you do, do not stay in an unproductive state of mind

Put worry and frustration aside

Success and failure are in the words that you speak

Discouragement will bind your feet

Proceed with grace to your desired place

You can climb if you wish, but mountains will move

Only you can determine the amount of faith used

Never Cease to Pray

*He takes me through a tunnel,
there is a light at the end*

*He gave me covering through the
storm, on God's protection I can
depend*

*Even when the clouds loom and the
sun does not shine*

*He fills my heart with tranquility
until new hope arrives*

*God our, defender, lover, and
friend*

*I thank you for never letting me
lose sight, placing it in my heart to
win*

*I will continue to bless the Lord
through whatever comes my way*

*He will answer if I never cease to
pray*

Never Stop

Never stop to concentrate on lack

*What you give out will definitely
come back*

*Take care of the small things if you
want more*

*If you appreciate what you have,
greater things are in store*

*Be anxious for nothing, your needs
are already counted*

*Worry is not profitable, through
gratitude, more is gained*

*Don't be the cause of your own
unnecessary pain*

*Our due diligence is what's
required, the results are beyond
our control*

Work towards enrichment,

Never stop to concentrate on lack

*For, what you give out will
definitely come back*

New Day

Arise with jubilation, a new day has come

Laughter fills my spirit tranquility is in the air

The stillness of God is everywhere

Today is a chance to remedy your past

An opportunity to reach for and task grasp

Every splendor that awaits is according to your faith

The old is passed away, we are beginning new

With different song and different tune

New Hope

*As the beat of my heart leaps,
there's a new passion inside of me*

*New hope birthed from a mount of
destruction,*

favor from destitution

Your presence is never an illusion

Ever-present is peace

*Our feet may be entangled, but
only for a short moment*

As we open our eyes to your grace,

the snare is undone and we step

into a new place

*The fulfillment of your promise, no
longer hostage to our limits,*

*but children of God, heir to his
privilege*

Now is the Time

Through good and bad times, you
can make it

Not by your power, but that which
is from above

Let your light shine and display lots
of love

It will become easy to ignore the
nay-say

Just depend on God and let him
have his way

The odds may not only be against
you, but stacked up high

Be determined to win and reach for
the sky

We are never promised another
day

Now is the time to say what you
are supposed to say

The week is almost through

Have you done what you were called to do?

One Thing

*Find one thing to be thankful for,
even though there are many more*

*As you think of that one, the rest
will flow*

Negativity has no choice but to go

*Fill your spirit with happiness and
cheer, your day will be much easier
to bear*

*Thankfulness brings joy to the
heart, even if everything around
you is falling apart*

*Keep a smile on your face and let a
song come from your mouth*

Wash away all worry and doubt

*Find one little thing to be thankful
for*

*You will remind yourself that there
are many more*

Patience

Those who have mercy, obtain much

Those who have been forgiven, forgive much

Patience is a component of love

Why spend years standing at the door, while you should be working to achieve more?

When you have relentlessly tried, you will be at peace

In your heart there will be a much earned release

It is better to walk through a door when it is open,

Plowing it down may cause a lifetime of regretting and hoping

Peace

The peace of a dove endows those
with love

Anger subsides when we realize
that it does not change a thing, but
poisons your very being

Laugh, smile, show kindness to
someone else

You no longer have time to rail and
pity yourself

You are the one with the choice
whether to overlook hostility or to
get on board

Live and walk in harmony,

endowed with love and the peace
of a dove

Peace Be Still

Peace be still and fill the air

Remove that which is heavy, calm every flutter

Substitute peace for a mind filled with clutter

Every spirit of war, we apprehend

Let newness of mind and serenity arise within

As we prepare for a fruitful day, our minds are focused

Our thoughts will not stray, far from the peace that fills the air

Our spirits filled with laughter and joy with no care

Perfection

There is a perfection that is greater
than man's

It does not seek vain glory or
applause, nor does it desire the
approval of all

This perfection is always on duty,
seeks to serve, and constantly
learns

A perfection that cannot be seen or
touched, it occurs within your spirit
and requires much

This perfection cannot be bought or
sold, but once obtained, is more
precious than rare stones

More coveted than beauty, rarely
found on a cover,

Favored above all transforming the
lives of others

Perfection of Love

Perfection of love is a key

It will take you to the places that you need to be

Be consistent no matter who is around

Disloyalty will cause you to lose respect and ground

Everyone needs someone to count on

Be an image of Christ on earth and stand strong

Our circumstances may change just as the wind,

however, that is not the characteristic of a true friend

Perfection of love is the key

Have courage, let it take you to where you need to be

Praises

Even birds sing praises to our Lord

For those in his image, it should be an automatic thing, to wake up and bless the Lord, King of Kings

Not taking for granted that he gave you breath and victory through the night over death

An inanimate object could take your place, but he keeps you covered by his grace

He's well overqualified and worthy of our praise

Open your eyes and begin to see, all of the things that you have undeservedly

They are not by chance or your own might, but by he who gives you the strength to fight

Prevailing

Move us, shake us

Mold us, make us persistently into
all that you have intended

With our minds surrendered, we
become humble before you so that
we may be lifted

Keep us firmly in your grasp so
that we may not slip or plummet

Let us rest securely in our being

Not doubting, but believing in the
faithfulness of one

With divine knowledge and
understanding we press for the
mark

Never failing, but prevailing

Positive Change

There is a connection between happiness and pain

Pain causes growth and positive change

Happiness is to be gained, by venturing into the unknown and defying old ways

The best and the worse may sometimes be the same

It may sound strange, but such is life

Go forth with purpose and there is no room for blame, only accountability to make a great name

Remain in good standing and let your blessings rain

The movement of the almighty, too much to tame

Don't be afraid of the pain, through it comes all positive change

Purpose

*In life we have setbacks, but what
we dwell on lingers*

*It's best not to waste our precious
moments being chased by ghosts*

*Take the good away from the bad
and call it growth*

*The knowledge that we gain makes
the unpleasant worthwhile,*

*creating happier times in the future
and wisdom to give our child*

*If we apply today our lessons from
the day before, we would
constantly flourish*

*Over-reaching our own
expectations with the abundance to*

*nourish the people and things that
have been placed into our lives*

bringing purpose to both us and them

and then suddenly, it will all make sense

Renewed

I will walk in the newness of life

*The light of the sun has shined
upon me*

*My weary heart is filled with
gladness*

I rise above all circumstances

*The richness of glory is like a river
flowing bountifully through me*

*There is no end in sight, I bubble
over with courage and might*

Joy and serenity possess my mind

*I am made in his image, yet one of
a kind*

Right Decisions

Good conscience leads you in the right direction

Move as quickly as you think

Don't give yourself time to blink

If you do, you will miss the ball every time

Make decisions according to your conviction

Allowing doubt to creep in, will rob you of your win

Rise Above

*Turn away from the old and flow
with what is new*

The best is still ahead of you

*Disentangled, yet surrendered,
give more than your all*

Get up and rise above if you fall

*Endurance is more important than
speed*

*Patience is the only thing that you
need*

*If all of your trust is in the right
place,*

*you are guaranteed to succeed in
every race*

Ruler of My Heart

The depth of my soul cries out for
thee

Ruler of my heart, source of
everything

There is no comparison for your
grace,

no substitute for your loving
kindness

I abandon myself and return all
that I am to you

The author and finisher of my faith

Allow you to guide me every step
of the way

Through the twists and the turns,
around the holes and snares

Submitting to your kindness,
knowing that you care

You have in store what is greatest for me

Ruler of my heart, source of everything

Run or Stand

*It may be dark for a season, but
the light will come*

Will you run or stand?

Are you working or sitting?

Will you be walking or just talking?

Are your hands clean or dirty?

Is your garment white or spotted?

The light will come at its due time

Will you run, or will you stand?

Seek After Peace

I seek after peace, my mind is content

My path is made straight and my destination aligned

My words are chosen and fall in line

That which is honorable, I will not undermine

My victory is already set

My joy will alleviate every bit of turmoil meant to deviate and paralyze my purpose

I will continue to move forward and seek after peace

My mind is at rest and my heart at ease

Sound of Peace

The beauty of the sound of peace
echoes in my spirit,

overshadowing the protests against
pacification

Undefeated harmonies willfully
drown the flirtation of fear

Enduring the urge to conform to
the simple,

exploring the depths of that which
is unidentifiable yet felt within

There is only a matter of time
before what is inside, will be
revealed with brightness just as a
light

The reign of darkness will end,
freeing tormented souls suffering
in silence

No longer violated

The beauty of the sound of peace
will echo for all to hear

Lingering in their spirits, breaking
down barriers that were created by
defeat

Stand

*Joy like a river flows from the heart
of the faithful*

*The virtue of love is like wellness
to the bones*

*Through them, beauty of the
perfect light is shown*

*The air that they breathe is fresh
as that of a tall green field*

Every desire of the mind fulfilled

Their soul rests in supple hands

*Through the violence surrounding
them, they stand*

*Conquering the contrary with
dominion and might*

*Razing and sending every enemy
to flight*

The Truth

The search for truth is a never
ending quest

Living your truth separates you
from the rest

Acknowledging your faults will help
you not to repeat

Reminding yourself of what is right
gives you the audacity to defeat

We will not fix what we won't admit

The truth is a friend to our destiny
and encourages us not to quit

No matter what you think, you are
able to succeed

Embrace truth and allow it to make
you free

There's More

Cultivate what comes naturally and watch it expand

Be willing to release what is in the confines of your hand

In order to receive, you have to give

Speak life to others and you will live

Bad seeds don't produce good fruit

So, kill all bitterness from its root

Knowledge is power and so is peace

All wrath and negativity must be released

You are a product of what you think

Keep your thoughts pure and only goodness will be reaped

*Every day is a blessing, one
greater than the day before*

*Make the best of it and believe that
there's more*

This Race

*Tomorrow is not promised, live
with no regrets*

*Every day as an adventure, still
looking forward to what's next*

*Only our Creator knows what we
have in store, so follow His lead*

*Full of optimism and confidence
that you will succeed*

*Keep your head up no matter what
opposition you face*

*Not swiftness, but steadiness
always wins this race*

True to Yourself

Be true to yourself and all that you are

Acknowledge your good traits and examine every flaw

Seek not only to look exemplary, but to be so

Beauty starts inside and radiates a glow

Your eyes are a window to the goodness within

Preserve their clarity, honesty is the best route to prosperity

If you end up in a state of disarray, recover quickly and find the right way

Be true to yourself and all that you are

Your uniqueness is a resource that will take you very far

Trust

Passion keeps a fire burning inside
of me

In spite of the obstacles that I
face, I know that I'm heading
towards the right place

How do I reach my destination?
One step at a time

I cannot move forward by standing
still

As I take each step, more and
more will be revealed

I trust in the perfect will of God,
placing my life in his hands

Surrendering to his plans and
falling in line

I know that they are greater than
mine

Undefeated

Be unapologetic for the grace on your life, unwilling to step back and dim your light

Even though you may be uncertain about the future that lies ahead, be unrelenting about what has already been said

The joy deep inside of you is unfeigned, unfounded due to the circumstances

Not easily understood to most

However, it's not unreachable unless you underestimate the importance of underlying values

that make you unbreakable in unacceptable conditions

Realize that you are never unguarded and don't become unfurled

*Remain unceasing and unshakable
in this uncivil world*

Wind of Glory

Just as the howling wind, your glory fills the room

I feel the sun, though it is not present

I hear God's voice, though I cannot see

The abundance of His charity encloses me

I lose myself to enter in and be captivated by your presence

Your sweet Spirit is a pleasant aroma, more satisfying than an expensive perfume

I apologize for my countenance, I would like to greet you with a smile

Then you told me that I must be broken to enter, so I will continue to bow

Just to feel the wind of your glory,

releasing all fear

*Having the comfort of knowing that
God is near*

The Wind

Push me as the wind does as sail

Guide me in the midst of turbulent tides

While I am in the ocean, grant me the tranquility of a gentle spring

There is no shore in sight

On the darkest night, you are my only light

I will rely on you entirely even when the day breaks and the others are finally awake

The wind in my sail, even when the sky is still

All of my hopes are fulfilled

Wings of Steel

My heart has wings of steel

It soars above all heaviness, not to be weighed down by the winds of change nor storms of opposition

My heart flies freely as if it were on the path of least resistance

It rests on clouds, love is abound and the resource of my force

I will not come down, but float at eagle's altitude

Sometimes you win, sometimes you lose, but my heart has wings of steel

My attitude is not determined by how I feel

Your Perfect Love

*You love us with a perfect love,
beyond understanding*

Immeasurable and selfless

*In the palm of your hand you hold
us, your words alone console us*

*Your love brings liberty and life to
a world full of strife*

*Peace where there is turmoil,
beauty where there are ashes*

Restoration where we are depleted

*Those who seek your face are not
defeated, but the children of your
promise*

*We are contagious, spreading your
perfect love*

EPILOGUE

*I have so many things to be
thankful for, how can I be silent?*

*Why wouldn't I listen when you
speak? Your insight is above all*

*I submit my existence to the
pioneer of life, you have observed
in entirety*

*I find refuge in your prophetic
words*

*I have done all that I can to stand,
leaving every battle in God's hands*

*The night hours are limited,
morning is soon to come*

*Let the perfect will of the Lord be
done*

**Dedicated to Dr. Maya Angelou
April 4, 1928-May 28, 2014**

Made in the USA
Lexington, KY
31 March 2017